50 Homemade Granola and Cereal Bars Recipes

By: Kelly Johnson

Table of Contents

- Classic Oatmeal Granola Bars
- Peanut Butter Chocolate Chip Bars
- Almond Joy Granola Bars
- Cinnamon Raisin Granola Bars
- No-Bake Coconut Almond Bars
- Honey and Almond Cereal Bars
- Dark Chocolate and Sea Salt Granola Bars
- Peanut Butter Banana Granola Bars
- Cherry and Pistachio Granola Bars
- Apple Cinnamon Oat Bars
- Tropical Fruit and Nut Granola Bars
- Protein-Packed Almond Butter Bars
- Maple Pecan Granola Bars
- Pumpkin Spice Granola Bars
- Coconut Cranberry Oat Bars
- Chocolate Coconut Granola Bars
- Raisin and Cashew Granola Bars
- Blueberry Oatmeal Bars
- Trail Mix Granola Bars
- Chocolate Peanut Butter Protein Bars
- Date and Cashew Energy Bars
- Apple Almond Granola Bars
- Apricot Walnut Granola Bars
- Strawberry and Coconut Granola Bars
- Coconut Chia Seed Bars
- Crunchy Granola Bars with Chia
- Caramelized Banana Granola Bars
- Dark Chocolate and Hazelnut Bars
- Strawberry Almond Butter Cereal Bars
- Maple Walnut Granola Bars
- Apple Cinnamon Crunch Bars
- Sweet and Salty Granola Bars
- Tropical Mango Cashew Granola Bars
- Chocolate Mint Granola Bars
- Cinnamon Pecan Oat Bars

- Trail Mix Granola Bars with Pretzels
- Peanut Butter and Jelly Granola Bars
- Lemon Poppy Seed Granola Bars
- Mocha Chocolate Granola Bars
- Cinnamon Sugar Granola Bars
- Raisin Bran Cereal Bars
- Pistachio Cherry Granola Bars
- Chocolate Almond Butter Protein Bars
- Blueberry Coconut Granola Bars
- Cranberry Almond Protein Bars
- Banana Walnut Granola Bars
- Gingerbread Granola Bars
- Salted Caramel Chocolate Granola Bars
- Matcha Green Tea Granola Bars
- Chocolate Hazelnut Oat Bars

Classic Oatmeal Granola Bars

Ingredients:

- 2 cups rolled oats
- 1/2 cup honey
- 1/4 cup peanut butter
- 1/4 cup brown sugar
- 1/4 cup milk
- 1 tsp vanilla extract
- 1/2 tsp cinnamon
- 1/4 tsp salt

Instructions:

1. **Prepare the Mixture**: In a medium saucepan, combine honey, peanut butter, brown sugar, milk, vanilla extract, cinnamon, and salt. Heat over medium heat, stirring until the sugar dissolves and the mixture is smooth.
2. **Combine with Oats**: Pour the mixture over the rolled oats and stir to combine.
3. **Press and Chill**: Line a baking dish with parchment paper and press the granola mixture into the dish. Refrigerate for at least 1 hour before cutting into bars.

Peanut Butter Chocolate Chip Bars

Ingredients:

- 1 cup peanut butter
- 1/2 cup honey
- 1/2 cup rolled oats
- 1/4 cup mini chocolate chips
- 1/4 tsp vanilla extract
- 1/4 tsp salt

Instructions:

1. **Mix Wet Ingredients**: In a saucepan, combine peanut butter and honey over low heat, stirring until smooth.
2. **Combine Dry Ingredients**: In a bowl, mix rolled oats, mini chocolate chips, vanilla extract, and salt.
3. **Combine and Chill**: Pour the peanut butter mixture into the dry ingredients and stir until well combined. Press the mixture into a baking dish and refrigerate for 1 hour. Cut into bars.

Almond Joy Granola Bars

Ingredients:

- 1 cup rolled oats
- 1/2 cup shredded coconut
- 1/4 cup almonds, chopped
- 1/4 cup chocolate chips
- 1/2 cup honey
- 1/4 cup almond butter
- 1 tsp vanilla extract
- 1/4 tsp salt

Instructions:

1. **Prepare the Mixture**: In a saucepan, combine honey and almond butter. Heat until smooth and combined.
2. **Mix with Dry Ingredients**: In a bowl, combine oats, shredded coconut, chopped almonds, chocolate chips, and salt.
3. **Press and Chill**: Pour the wet mixture into the dry ingredients and stir to combine. Press into a baking dish and refrigerate for 1 hour. Cut into bars.

Cinnamon Raisin Granola Bars

Ingredients:

- 2 cups rolled oats
- 1/2 cup raisins
- 1/4 cup honey
- 1/4 cup almond butter
- 1/2 tsp cinnamon
- 1/4 tsp vanilla extract
- 1/4 tsp salt

Instructions:

1. **Heat Wet Ingredients**: In a saucepan, combine honey, almond butter, cinnamon, and vanilla extract. Heat over medium heat until smooth.
2. **Combine with Dry Ingredients**: In a large bowl, mix the oats, raisins, and salt. Pour the wet mixture over and stir to combine.
3. **Press and Chill**: Press the mixture into a lined baking dish. Refrigerate for at least 1 hour before cutting into bars.

No-Bake Coconut Almond Bars

Ingredients:

- 1 cup shredded coconut
- 1/2 cup almonds, chopped
- 1/2 cup honey
- 1/4 cup almond butter
- 1 tsp vanilla extract

Instructions:

1. **Combine Ingredients**: In a bowl, combine shredded coconut, chopped almonds, honey, almond butter, and vanilla extract. Stir until everything is well coated.
2. **Press and Chill**: Press the mixture into a lined baking dish and refrigerate for 1 hour. Slice into bars.

Honey and Almond Cereal Bars

Ingredients:

- 2 cups rice cereal
- 1/2 cup chopped almonds
- 1/4 cup honey
- 1/4 cup almond butter
- 1/4 tsp vanilla extract
- 1/4 tsp salt

Instructions:

1. **Heat Wet Ingredients**: In a saucepan, heat honey and almond butter until smooth and well combined.
2. **Mix with Dry Ingredients**: In a bowl, mix rice cereal, chopped almonds, vanilla extract, and salt. Pour the wet mixture over and stir to combine.
3. **Press and Chill**: Press the mixture into a lined baking dish. Refrigerate for 1 hour, then cut into bars.

Dark Chocolate and Sea Salt Granola Bars

Ingredients:

- 2 cups rolled oats
- 1/2 cup dark chocolate chips
- 1/4 cup honey
- 1/4 cup almond butter
- 1 tsp vanilla extract
- 1/4 tsp sea salt

Instructions:

1. **Heat Wet Ingredients**: In a saucepan, combine honey, almond butter, and vanilla extract. Heat over low heat until smooth.
2. **Mix with Dry Ingredients**: In a bowl, combine oats, dark chocolate chips, and sea salt. Pour the wet mixture over and stir to combine.
3. **Press and Chill**: Press into a lined baking dish and refrigerate for 1 hour. Cut into bars.

Peanut Butter Banana Granola Bars

Ingredients:

- 1 1/2 cups rolled oats
- 1/2 cup peanut butter
- 1/4 cup honey
- 1/2 ripe banana, mashed
- 1/4 cup mini chocolate chips
- 1/4 tsp vanilla extract
- 1/4 tsp salt

Instructions:

1. **Mash Banana**: In a bowl, mash the ripe banana.
2. **Combine Ingredients**: Stir in peanut butter, honey, vanilla extract, and salt. Add oats and chocolate chips, mixing until well combined.
3. **Press and Chill**: Press the mixture into a lined baking dish and refrigerate for at least 1 hour before cutting into bars.

Cherry and Pistachio Granola Bars

Ingredients:

- 1 cup rolled oats
- 1/2 cup dried cherries
- 1/2 cup pistachios, chopped
- 1/4 cup honey
- 1/4 cup almond butter
- 1 tsp vanilla extract
- 1/4 tsp salt
  Instructions:
1. **Combine Wet Ingredients**: Heat honey and almond butter until smooth.
2. **Mix with Dry Ingredients**: Stir in oats, cherries, pistachios, vanilla, and salt.
3. **Press and Chill**: Press into a dish, refrigerate for 1 hour, and cut into bars.

Apple Cinnamon Oat Bars

Ingredients:

- 2 cups rolled oats
- 1/2 cup dried apples, chopped
- 1/2 tsp cinnamon
- 1/4 cup honey
- 1/4 cup applesauce
- 1/4 cup almond butter

Instructions:

1. **Heat Wet Ingredients**: Combine honey, applesauce, and almond butter, heating until smooth.
2. **Combine with Dry Ingredients**: Mix oats, apples, and cinnamon.
3. **Press and Chill**: Press into a dish, refrigerate for 1 hour, and cut into bars.

Tropical Fruit and Nut Granola Bars

Ingredients:

- 2 cups rolled oats
- 1/2 cup dried mango
- 1/4 cup cashews, chopped
- 1/4 cup coconut flakes
- 1/4 cup honey
- 1/4 cup almond butter

Instructions:

1. **Combine Wet Ingredients**: Heat honey and almond butter until smooth.
2. **Mix with Dry Ingredients**: Stir in oats, mango, cashews, and coconut.
3. **Press and Chill**: Press into a dish, refrigerate for 1 hour, and cut into bars.

Protein-Packed Almond Butter Bars

Ingredients:

- 2 cups rolled oats
- 1/2 cup almond butter
- 1/4 cup honey
- 1/4 cup protein powder
- 1/4 tsp vanilla extract
  Instructions:
1. **Heat Wet Ingredients**: Combine almond butter and honey, heating until smooth.
2. **Mix with Dry Ingredients**: Stir in oats, protein powder, and vanilla.
3. **Press and Chill**: Press into a dish, refrigerate for 1 hour, and cut into bars.

Maple Pecan Granola Bars

Ingredients:

- 2 cups rolled oats
- 1/2 cup pecans, chopped
- 1/4 cup maple syrup
- 1/4 cup almond butter
- 1 tsp vanilla extract

Instructions:

1. **Combine Wet Ingredients**: Heat maple syrup and almond butter until smooth.
2. **Mix with Dry Ingredients**: Stir in oats, pecans, and vanilla.
3. **Press and Chill**: Press into a dish, refrigerate for 1 hour, and cut into bars.

Pumpkin Spice Granola Bars

Ingredients:

- 2 cups rolled oats
- 1/4 cup pumpkin puree
- 1/4 cup honey
- 1/4 cup almond butter
- 1 tsp pumpkin spice
- 1/4 tsp vanilla extract

Instructions:

1. **Combine Wet Ingredients**: Heat honey, pumpkin puree, and almond butter until smooth.
2. **Mix with Dry Ingredients**: Stir in oats, pumpkin spice, and vanilla.
3. **Press and Chill**: Press into a dish, refrigerate for 1 hour, and cut into bars.

Coconut Cranberry Oat Bars

Ingredients:

- 2 cups rolled oats
- 1/2 cup dried cranberries
- 1/2 cup coconut flakes
- 1/4 cup honey
- 1/4 cup almond butter

Instructions:

1. **Combine Wet Ingredients**: Heat honey and almond butter until smooth.
2. **Mix with Dry Ingredients**: Stir in oats, cranberries, and coconut.
3. **Press and Chill**: Press into a dish, refrigerate for 1 hour, and cut into bars.

Chocolate Coconut Granola Bars

Ingredients:

- 2 cups rolled oats
- 1/2 cup coconut flakes
- 1/4 cup dark chocolate chips
- 1/4 cup honey
- 1/4 cup almond butter

Instructions:

1. **Combine Wet Ingredients**: Heat honey and almond butter until smooth.
2. **Mix with Dry Ingredients**: Stir in oats, coconut, and chocolate chips.
3. **Press and Chill**: Press into a dish, refrigerate for 1 hour, and cut into bars.

Raisin and Cashew Granola Bars

Ingredients:

- 2 cups rolled oats
- 1/2 cup raisins
- 1/4 cup cashews, chopped
- 1/4 cup honey
- 1/4 cup almond butter

Instructions:

1. **Combine Wet Ingredients**: Heat honey and almond butter until smooth.
2. **Mix with Dry Ingredients**: Stir in oats, raisins, and cashews.
3. **Press and Chill**: Press into a dish, refrigerate for 1 hour, and cut into bars.

Blueberry Oatmeal Bars

Ingredients:

- 2 cups rolled oats
- 1/2 cup dried blueberries
- 1/4 cup honey
- 1/4 cup almond butter
- 1/2 tsp vanilla extract
- 1/4 tsp salt

Instructions:

1. **Combine Wet Ingredients**: Heat honey and almond butter until smooth.
2. **Mix with Dry Ingredients**: Stir in oats, blueberries, vanilla, and salt.
3. **Press and Chill**: Press into a dish, refrigerate for 1 hour, and cut into bars.

Trail Mix Granola Bars

Ingredients:

- 2 cups rolled oats
- 1/4 cup sunflower seeds
- 1/4 cup pumpkin seeds
- 1/4 cup dried cranberries
- 1/4 cup almonds, chopped
- 1/4 cup honey
- 1/4 cup almond butter

Instructions:

1. **Combine Wet Ingredients**: Heat honey and almond butter until smooth.
2. **Mix with Dry Ingredients**: Stir in oats, seeds, cranberries, and almonds.
3. **Press and Chill**: Press into a dish, refrigerate for 1 hour, and cut into bars.

Chocolate Peanut Butter Protein Bars

Ingredients:

- 1 cup rolled oats
- 1/2 cup chocolate protein powder
- 1/4 cup peanut butter
- 1/4 cup honey
- 1/4 cup milk (or almond milk)
- 1/4 tsp vanilla extract

Instructions:

1. **Combine Wet Ingredients**: Heat peanut butter, honey, and milk until smooth.
2. **Mix with Dry Ingredients**: Stir in oats, protein powder, and vanilla.
3. **Press and Chill**: Press into a dish, refrigerate for 1 hour, and cut into bars.

Date and Cashew Energy Bars

Ingredients:

- 1 cup dates, pitted
- 1/2 cup cashews
- 1/4 cup rolled oats
- 2 tbsp honey
- 1/4 tsp vanilla extract

Instructions:

1. **Blend Dates and Cashews**: Blend dates, cashews, and oats in a food processor until finely chopped.
2. **Mix with Wet Ingredients**: Stir in honey and vanilla.
3. **Press and Chill**: Press into a dish, refrigerate for 1 hour, and cut into bars.

Apple Almond Granola Bars

Ingredients:

- 2 cups rolled oats
- 1/2 cup dried apples, chopped
- 1/4 cup almonds, chopped
- 1/4 cup honey
- 1/4 cup almond butter
- 1/2 tsp cinnamon

Instructions:

1. **Combine Wet Ingredients**: Heat honey and almond butter until smooth.
2. **Mix with Dry Ingredients**: Stir in oats, apples, almonds, and cinnamon.
3. **Press and Chill**: Press into a dish, refrigerate for 1 hour, and cut into bars.

Apricot Walnut Granola Bars

Ingredients:

- 2 cups rolled oats
- 1/2 cup dried apricots, chopped
- 1/4 cup walnuts, chopped
- 1/4 cup honey
- 1/4 cup almond butter

Instructions:

1. **Combine Wet Ingredients**: Heat honey and almond butter until smooth.
2. **Mix with Dry Ingredients**: Stir in oats, apricots, walnuts.
3. **Press and Chill**: Press into a dish, refrigerate for 1 hour, and cut into bars.

Strawberry and Coconut Granola Bars

Ingredients:

- 2 cups rolled oats
- 1/2 cup dried strawberries, chopped
- 1/4 cup shredded coconut
- 1/4 cup honey
- 1/4 cup almond butter

Instructions:

1. **Combine Wet Ingredients**: Heat honey and almond butter until smooth.
2. **Mix with Dry Ingredients**: Stir in oats, strawberries, and coconut.
3. **Press and Chill**: Press into a dish, refrigerate for 1 hour, and cut into bars.

Coconut Chia Seed Bars

Ingredients:

- 2 cups rolled oats
- 1/4 cup chia seeds
- 1/4 cup shredded coconut
- 1/4 cup honey
- 1/4 cup almond butter

Instructions:

1. **Combine Wet Ingredients**: Heat honey and almond butter until smooth.
2. **Mix with Dry Ingredients**: Stir in oats, chia seeds, and coconut.
3. **Press and Chill**: Press into a dish, refrigerate for 1 hour, and cut into bars.

Crunchy Granola Bars with Chia

Ingredients:

- 2 cups rolled oats
- 1/4 cup chia seeds
- 1/2 cup almonds, chopped
- 1/4 cup honey
- 1/4 cup peanut butter
- 1/2 tsp vanilla extract
   Instructions:
1. **Combine Wet Ingredients**: Heat honey and peanut butter until smooth.
2. **Mix with Dry Ingredients**: Stir in oats, chia seeds, and almonds.
3. **Press and Chill**: Press into a dish, refrigerate for 1 hour, and cut into bars.

Caramelized Banana Granola Bars

Ingredients:

- 2 ripe bananas, mashed
- 2 cups rolled oats
- 1/4 cup honey
- 1/4 cup peanut butter
- 1/4 tsp cinnamon
- 1/4 cup walnuts, chopped

Instructions:

1. **Caramelize Bananas**: Sauté mashed bananas in a pan over low heat until golden brown.
2. **Combine Wet Ingredients**: Mix honey and peanut butter, and add caramelized bananas.
3. **Mix with Dry Ingredients**: Stir in oats, cinnamon, and walnuts.
4. **Press and Chill**: Press into a dish, refrigerate for 1 hour, and cut into bars.

Dark Chocolate and Hazelnut Bars

Ingredients:

- 2 cups rolled oats
- 1/4 cup hazelnuts, chopped
- 1/4 cup dark chocolate chips
- 1/4 cup honey
- 1/4 cup almond butter

Instructions:

1. **Combine Wet Ingredients**: Heat honey and almond butter until smooth.
2. **Mix with Dry Ingredients**: Stir in oats, hazelnuts, and chocolate chips.
3. **Press and Chill**: Press into a dish, refrigerate for 1 hour, and cut into bars.

Strawberry Almond Butter Cereal Bars

Ingredients:

- 2 cups rolled oats
- 1/4 cup almond butter
- 1/4 cup freeze-dried strawberries, chopped
- 1/4 cup honey
- 1/4 tsp vanilla extract

Instructions:

1. **Combine Wet Ingredients**: Heat almond butter and honey until smooth.
2. **Mix with Dry Ingredients**: Stir in oats, freeze-dried strawberries, and vanilla.
3. **Press and Chill**: Press into a dish, refrigerate for 1 hour, and cut into bars.

Maple Walnut Granola Bars

Ingredients:

- 2 cups rolled oats
- 1/4 cup walnuts, chopped
- 1/4 cup maple syrup
- 1/4 cup almond butter
- 1/2 tsp cinnamon
  Instructions:
1. **Combine Wet Ingredients**: Heat maple syrup and almond butter until smooth.
2. **Mix with Dry Ingredients**: Stir in oats, walnuts, and cinnamon.
3. **Press and Chill**: Press into a dish, refrigerate for 1 hour, and cut into bars.

Apple Cinnamon Crunch Bars

Ingredients:

- 2 cups rolled oats
- 1/2 cup dried apples, chopped
- 1/4 tsp cinnamon
- 1/4 cup honey
- 1/4 cup almond butter

Instructions:

1. **Combine Wet Ingredients**: Heat honey and almond butter until smooth.
2. **Mix with Dry Ingredients**: Stir in oats, dried apples, and cinnamon.
3. **Press and Chill**: Press into a dish, refrigerate for 1 hour, and cut into bars.

Sweet and Salty Granola Bars

Ingredients:

- 2 cups rolled oats
- 1/4 cup sunflower seeds
- 1/4 cup pretzels, crushed
- 1/4 cup honey
- 1/4 cup almond butter
- 1/4 tsp sea salt

Instructions:

1. **Combine Wet Ingredients**: Heat honey and almond butter until smooth.
2. **Mix with Dry Ingredients**: Stir in oats, sunflower seeds, crushed pretzels, and sea salt.
3. **Press and Chill**: Press into a dish, refrigerate for 1 hour, and cut into bars.

Tropical Mango Cashew Granola Bars

Ingredients:

- 2 cups rolled oats
- 1/4 cup dried mango, chopped
- 1/4 cup cashews, chopped
- 1/4 cup honey
- 1/4 cup coconut oil

Instructions:

1. **Combine Wet Ingredients**: Heat honey and coconut oil until smooth.
2. **Mix with Dry Ingredients**: Stir in oats, dried mango, and cashews.
3. **Press and Chill**: Press into a dish, refrigerate for 1 hour, and cut into bars.

Chocolate Mint Granola Bars

Ingredients:

- 2 cups rolled oats
- 1/4 cup dark chocolate chips
- 1/4 cup peppermint extract
- 1/4 cup honey
- 1/4 cup almond butter

Instructions:

1. **Combine Wet Ingredients**: Heat honey, almond butter, and peppermint extract until smooth.
2. **Mix with Dry Ingredients**: Stir in oats and dark chocolate chips.
3. **Press and Chill**: Press into a dish, refrigerate for 1 hour, and cut into bars.

Cinnamon Pecan Oat Bars

Ingredients:

- 2 cups rolled oats
- 1/4 cup pecans, chopped
- 1/4 tsp cinnamon
- 1/4 cup honey
- 1/4 cup almond butter

Instructions:

1. **Combine Wet Ingredients**: Heat honey and almond butter until smooth.
2. **Mix with Dry Ingredients**: Stir in oats, pecans, and cinnamon.
3. **Press and Chill**: Press into a dish, refrigerate for 1 hour, and cut into bars.

Trail Mix Granola Bars with Pretzels

Ingredients:

- 2 cups rolled oats
- 1/4 cup pretzels, crushed
- 1/4 cup dried cranberries
- 1/4 cup sunflower seeds
- 1/4 cup honey
- 1/4 cup peanut butter

Instructions:

1. **Combine Wet Ingredients**: Heat honey and peanut butter until smooth.
2. **Mix with Dry Ingredients**: Stir in oats, crushed pretzels, dried cranberries, and sunflower seeds.
3. **Press and Chill**: Press into a dish, refrigerate for 1 hour, and cut into bars.

Peanut Butter and Jelly Granola Bars

Ingredients:

- 2 cups rolled oats
- 1/4 cup peanut butter
- 1/4 cup strawberry jam
- 1/4 cup honey
- 1/4 tsp vanilla extract

Instructions:

1. **Combine Wet Ingredients**: Heat honey, peanut butter, and vanilla extract until smooth.
2. **Mix with Dry Ingredients**: Stir in oats and strawberry jam.
3. **Press and Chill**: Press into a dish, refrigerate for 1 hour, and cut into bars.

Lemon Poppy Seed Granola Bars

Ingredients:

- 2 cups rolled oats
- 1 tbsp poppy seeds
- 1/4 cup lemon juice
- 1/4 cup honey
- 1/4 cup coconut oil

Instructions:

1. **Combine Wet Ingredients**: Heat honey, coconut oil, and lemon juice until smooth.
2. **Mix with Dry Ingredients**: Stir in oats and poppy seeds.
3. **Press and Chill**: Press into a dish, refrigerate for 1 hour, and cut into bars.

Mocha Chocolate Granola Bars

Ingredients:

- 2 cups rolled oats
- 1/4 cup dark chocolate chips
- 1 tbsp instant coffee granules
- 1/4 cup honey
- 1/4 cup almond butter

Instructions:

1. **Combine Wet Ingredients**: Heat honey, almond butter, and coffee granules until smooth.
2. **Mix with Dry Ingredients**: Stir in oats and dark chocolate chips.
3. **Press and Chill**: Press into a dish, refrigerate for 1 hour, and cut into bars.

Cinnamon Sugar Granola Bars

Ingredients:

- 2 cups rolled oats
- 1/4 cup sugar
- 1 tsp cinnamon
- 1/4 cup honey
- 1/4 cup almond butter

Instructions:

1. **Combine Wet Ingredients**: Heat honey and almond butter until smooth.
2. **Mix with Dry Ingredients**: Stir in oats, sugar, and cinnamon.
3. **Press and Chill**: Press into a dish, refrigerate for 1 hour, and cut into bars.

Raisin Bran Cereal Bars

Ingredients:

- 2 cups rolled oats
- 1 cup Raisin Bran cereal
- 1/4 cup honey
- 1/4 cup almond butter
- 1/4 tsp vanilla extract

Instructions:

1. **Combine Wet Ingredients**: Heat honey, almond butter, and vanilla extract until smooth.
2. **Mix with Dry Ingredients**: Stir in oats and Raisin Bran cereal.
3. **Press and Chill**: Press into a dish, refrigerate for 1 hour, and cut into bars.

Pistachio Cherry Granola Bars

Ingredients:

- 2 cups rolled oats
- 1/4 cup pistachios, chopped
- 1/4 cup dried cherries, chopped
- 1/4 cup honey
- 1/4 cup almond butter

Instructions:

1. **Combine Wet Ingredients**: Heat honey and almond butter until smooth.
2. **Mix with Dry Ingredients**: Stir in oats, pistachios, and dried cherries.
3. **Press and Chill**: Press into a dish, refrigerate for 1 hour, and cut into bars.

Chocolate Almond Butter Protein Bars

Ingredients:

- 2 cups rolled oats
- 1/4 cup chocolate protein powder
- 1/4 cup almond butter
- 1/4 cup honey
- 1/4 cup dark chocolate chips

Instructions:

1. **Combine Wet Ingredients**: Heat honey and almond butter until smooth.
2. **Mix with Dry Ingredients**: Stir in oats and protein powder.
3. **Fold in Chocolate Chips**: Stir in dark chocolate chips.
4. **Press and Chill**: Press into a dish, refrigerate for 1 hour, and cut into bars.

Blueberry Coconut Granola Bars

Ingredients:

- 2 cups rolled oats
- 1/4 cup shredded coconut
- 1/4 cup dried blueberries
- 1/4 cup honey
- 1/4 cup coconut oil

Instructions:

1. **Combine Wet Ingredients**: Heat honey and coconut oil until smooth.
2. **Mix with Dry Ingredients**: Stir in oats, shredded coconut, and dried blueberries.
3. **Press and Chill**: Press into a dish, refrigerate for 1 hour, and cut into bars.

Cranberry Almond Protein Bars

Ingredients:

- 2 cups rolled oats
- 1/4 cup dried cranberries
- 1/4 cup almond butter
- 1/4 cup honey
- 1/4 cup vanilla protein powder

Instructions:

1. **Combine Wet Ingredients**: Heat honey and almond butter until smooth.
2. **Mix with Dry Ingredients**: Stir in oats and protein powder.
3. **Fold in Cranberries**: Stir in dried cranberries.
4. **Press and Chill**: Press into a dish, refrigerate for 1 hour, and cut into bars.

Banana Walnut Granola Bars

Ingredients:

- 2 cups rolled oats
- 1/4 cup walnuts, chopped
- 1 ripe banana, mashed
- 1/4 cup honey
- 1/4 cup almond butter

Instructions:

1. **Combine Wet Ingredients**: Mash banana and heat honey and almond butter until smooth.
2. **Mix with Dry Ingredients**: Stir in oats and walnuts.
3. **Press and Chill**: Press into a dish, refrigerate for 1 hour, and cut into bars.

Gingerbread Granola Bars

Ingredients:

- 2 cups rolled oats
- 1/4 tsp ground ginger
- 1/4 tsp cinnamon
- 1/4 cup molasses
- 1/4 cup honey
- 1/4 cup almond butter

Instructions:

1. **Combine Wet Ingredients**: Heat molasses, honey, and almond butter until smooth.
2. **Mix with Dry Ingredients**: Stir in oats, ground ginger, and cinnamon.
3. **Press and Chill**: Press into a dish, refrigerate for 1 hour, and cut into bars.

Salted Caramel Chocolate Granola Bars

Ingredients:

- 2 cups rolled oats
- 1/4 cup caramel sauce
- 1/4 cup dark chocolate chips
- 1/4 tsp sea salt
- 1/4 cup almond butter

Instructions:

1. **Combine Wet Ingredients**: Heat caramel sauce and almond butter until smooth.
2. **Mix with Dry Ingredients**: Stir in oats and dark chocolate chips.
3. **Press and Chill**: Press into a dish, sprinkle with sea salt, refrigerate for 1 hour, and cut into bars.

Matcha Green Tea Granola Bars

Ingredients:

- 2 cups rolled oats
- 1 tbsp matcha powder
- 1/4 cup honey
- 1/4 cup almond butter
- 1/4 cup shredded coconut

Instructions:

1. **Combine Wet Ingredients**: Heat honey and almond butter until smooth.
2. **Mix with Dry Ingredients**: Stir in oats, matcha powder, and shredded coconut.
3. **Press and Chill**: Press into a dish, refrigerate for 1 hour, and cut into bars.

Chocolate Hazelnut Oat Bars

Ingredients:

- 2 cups rolled oats
- 1/4 cup chocolate hazelnut spread
- 1/4 cup honey
- 1/4 cup chopped hazelnuts
- 1/4 cup almond butter

Instructions:

1. **Combine Wet Ingredients**: Heat honey, almond butter, and chocolate hazelnut spread until smooth.
2. **Mix with Dry Ingredients**: Stir in oats and chopped hazelnuts.
3. **Press and Chill**: Press into a dish, refrigerate for 1 hour, and cut into bars.

www.ingramcontent.com/pod-product-compliance
Lightning Source LLC
LaVergne TN
LVHW061955070526
838199LV00060B/4125